A LIGHT *for the* JOURNEY

...Mobile Bay...

D. Morgan®

HARVEST HOUSE PUBLISHERS

Eugene, Oregon

A LIGHT for the JOURNEY

Text Copyright © 2001 by Harvest House Publishers
Eugene, Oregon 97402

ISBN 0-7369-0570-7

Artwork designs are reproduced under license from
Arts Uniq', Inc., Cookeville, TN and may not be
reproduced without permission. For information
regarding art prints featured in this book, please contact:

Arts Uniq'
P.O. Box 3085
Cookeville, TN 38502
1.800.223.5020

Design and production by Koechel Peterson and Associates
Minneapolis, Minnesota

Harvest House Publishers has made every effort to trace the ownership of all poems and quotes. In
the event of a question arising from the use of a poem or quote, we regret any error made and will be
pleased to make the necessary correction in future editions of this book.

"The Lighthouse" by Ronnie Hinson © 1971 Dayspring Music, Inc. and Songs of Calvary Music.
All rights reserved. Used by permission. International rights secured.

Scripture quotations are taken from the Holy Bible, New International Version®, Copyright © 1973,
1978, 1984 by the International Bible Society. Used by permission of Zondervan Publishing House.

Printed in China.

01 02 03 04 05 06 07 08 09 10 / IM / 10 9 8 7 6 5 4 3 2 1

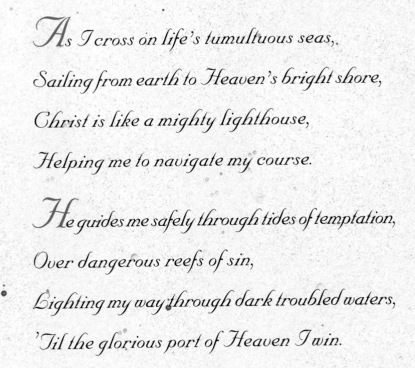

D. Morgan

As I cross on life's tumultuous seas,

Sailing from earth to Heaven's bright shore,

Christ is like a mighty lighthouse,

Helping me to navigate my course.

He guides me safely through tides of temptation,

Over dangerous reefs of sin,

Lighting my way through dark troubled waters,

'Til the glorious port of Heaven I win.

Author Unknown

There's a lighthouse on the hillside that overlooks life's sea. When I'm tossed, it sends out a light that I might see. And the light that shines in darkness now will safely lead us o'er. If it wasn't for the lighthouse, my ship would be no more.

Ronnie Hinson

A tower of strength
Through darkest night
    Classic beauty...

    ...St. Augustine Light

Meanwhile the lighthouse had been

growing slowly larger. It had now

almost assumed colour, and appeared

like a little grey shadow on the sky.

Stephen Crane

Linger by the sea, where worldly cares are few.

The ship was cheer'd, the harbour clear'd,
Merrily did we drop
Below the kirk, below the hill,
Below the lighthouse top.
The Sun came up upon the left,
Out of the sea came he!
And he shone bright, and on the right
Went down into the sea.

Samuel Taylor Coleridge

*The great revolving light on the
cliff at the channel flashed warm
and golden against the clear
northern sky, a trembling,
quivering star of good hope.*

L. M. Montgomery
Anne's House of Dreams

I am the light of the world. Whoever follows me will never walk in darkness, but will have the light of life.

The Book of John

St. Simons Island Light

This regal Towering giant
Made the dark horizon bright
On the coast of Georgia...

D. Morgan ® © 2000

Now the rolling of the
billows I can hear,
As they beat on the turf
bound shore;
But the beacon light of love
so bright and clear,
Guides my bark, frail and
lone, safely over.
And no evil will I fear while
my Shepherd is so near,
There's a light in the valley
for me.

P. P. Bliss

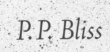

A great lighthouse
which stands there,
Flashing out beams of light,
Indifferent to the waves
which beat against him.

~

Roy Jenkins

Your lantern shining bright
High above the churning waves
Oregons jewel ...
... Heceta
Head

Lovely lady of the sea

D. Morgan® © 2000

Light

I like to think of hope as a guiding light for the human heart. It is the quality that will help you find your way through dark and stormy nights, through foggy and confusing days.

Thomas Kinkade

*It is during our darkest moments
that we must focus to see the light.*

Taylor Benson

D. Morgan

The Lord is my light
and my salvation—
whom shall I fear?
The Lord is the
stronghold of my life—
of whom shall I be afraid?

The Book of Psalms

A sentinel of solitude
Once lit the sailors way
This light in Alabama
Saved in ....

We judge by certain laws and principles, and feel tolerably safe about the structure; but, after all, we shall know best if after-years when a thousand tempests have beaten upon the lighthouse in vain. We need trials as a test as much as we need divine truth as our food.

Charles Spurgeon

...Mobile Bay.

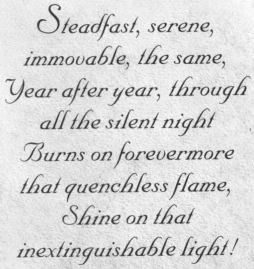

Steadfast, serene,
immovable, the same,
Year after year, through
all the silent night
Burns on forevermore
that quenchless flame,
Shine on that
inextinguishable light!

Henry Wadsworth Longfellow
"The Lighthouse"

On windswept shores
Of Lake Michigan
Seawatch of the night

Lighthouses don't fire cannons to
call attention to their shining.
They just shine.

D.L. Moody

D. Morgan © 2000

all   and proud . . .

Little Sable Point Light

*Over the noise
of the angry storm,
I heard Him call
my name.
"You are hidden with me—
safe in My care
From eternity to eternity—
I am the same."*

Margaret Jensen

Begin today!
No matter how
feeble the light,
let it shine
as best it may.
The world may need
just that quality
of light which you have.

Henry C. Blinn

Strong as thunder
In the night
Hatteras...
You Grand Old
Light.

Your transforming faith in Me cannot be crushed but instead shines like a lighthouse, drawing those who sincerely search for the Way, the Truth, and the Life.

Steve Haas

D. Morgan © 2000

In Him was life, and that life was the light of men.

The Book of John

From the Heritage of Sea Pines
To Calibogue Sound
That old familiar greeting

D. Morgan © 2000

The light...

I have come into the world as a light, so that no one who believes in me should stay in darkness.

The Book of John

... At Harbour Town

The light that shines from the crucified
is a light...which both illuminates the
obscurity of being and overcomes the
darkness of nonbeing.

Nicholas Berdyaev

D. Morgan

Light is the symbol of truth.

James Russell Lowell

...God, as promised,
proves to be mercy
clothed in light.

Jane Kenyon

There are two kinds of light—
the glow that illumines, and
the glare that obscures.

James Thurber

The scene was more
beautiful far to the eye,
Than if the day in its pride
had arrayed it.
And o'er them the
lighthouse looked lovely
as hope—
That star of life's
tremulous ocean.

Paul Moon James

A mighty gale   took the Big

On that "Witch

Nothing coul

Not

tity) down

of "November" night.

ave her from perilous fate

en . . .

. . . Majestic
Split Rock Light.

And it isn't any hurricane that
could put its light out, though,
it should blow from all points
of the compass at once! Ships
will see it in time to get their
bearings. They will find their
way by its light, and they won't
be in danger of running onto
the rocks . . .

Jules Verne
Lighthouse at the End of the World

He who appoints the sun to shine by day,
who decrees the moon and stars to shine by night,
who stirs up the sea so that its waves roar—
the Lord Almighty is his name.

The Book of Jeremiah

D. Morgan

There are two ways of
spreading light: To be the candle
or the mirror that reflects it.

Edith Wharton

May our hearts make Jesus their anchor, their rudder, their lighthouse, their life-boat, and their harbour. His Church is the Admiral's flagship; let us attend her movements, and cheer her officers with our presence. He Himself is the great attraction; let us follow ever in His wake, mark His signals, steer by His chart, and never fear while He is within hail. Not one ship in the convoy shall suffer wreck; the great Commodore will steer every barque in safety to the desired haven. By faith we will slip our cable for another day's cruise, and sail forth with Jesus into a sea of tribulation. Winds and waves will not spare us, but they all obey Him; and, therefore, whatever squalls may occur without, faith shall feel a blessed calm within. He is ever in the centre of the weather-beaten company: let us rejoice in Him. His vessel has reached the haven, and so shall ours.

Charles Spurgeon

Brightly beams our
   Father's mercy
From His lighthouse evermore,
But to us He gives the keeping
Of the lights along the shore.

Let the lower lights be burning!
Send a gleam across the wave!
Some poor fainting,
   struggling seaman
You may rescue, you may save.

P.P. Bliss

When the light has sharply faded
And you have lost your way
Let another's love guide you
It can turn blackest night into day.

Kevin Meyers

D. Morgan © 1998

You are the light of the world, but the switch must be turned on.

Austin Alexander Lewis

*J*ust think of the illimitable abundance
and the marvelous loveliness of light,
or of the beauty of the sun
and moon and stars.

Saint Augustine

Lighthouse beacon in the night.

May the blessing of light be on you,

light without and light within.

May the blessed sunshine shine on your

land, warm your heart....

Traditional Irish Blessing

D. Morgan © 1994

Lead, kindly Light, amid
th' encircling gloom, lead
Thou me on!
The night is dark, and I
am far from home; lead
Thou me on!
Keep Thou my feet;
I do not ask to see
The distant scene; one
step enough for me.

John Henry Newman
"Lead, Kindly Light"

Many an ancient mariner
Survived the storms of night
Majestic Point
Bonita . . .

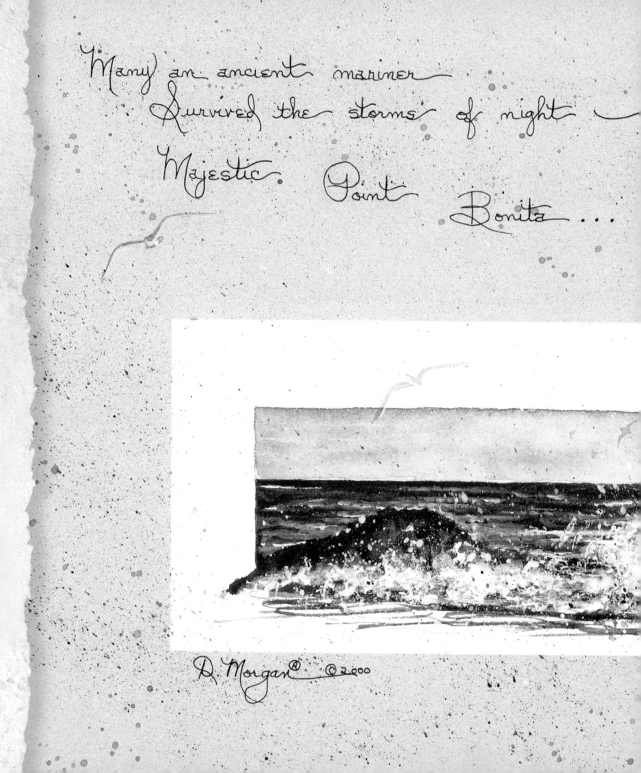

D. Morgan® ©2000

Of men and boats and
harbors from the storm,
the Lighthouse brings them
back to shore
Like a beacon in the night,
guide us to the light.

Michael Goodwin

Gracious Saving Light

God does not give heed to the
ambitiousness of our prayers, because
He is always ready to give to us His
light, not a visible light but an
intellectual and spiritual one...

Saint Augustine

A sailor's answered prayer in sight ~
This shining fortress...

... Highland Light.

Darkness cannot drive
out darkness; only
light can do that. Hate
cannot drive out hate;
only love can do that.

Martin Luther King, Jr.

D. Morgan® ©2000

From San Francisco to
This beauty lights

His light, through me,

will glow as a beacon

for others.

John C. Thibos

San Pablo
the way

A ship on the beach
is a lighthouse to the sea.
Dutch Proverb

D. Morgan © 2000

East Brother Light
...Landmark
By The Bay.

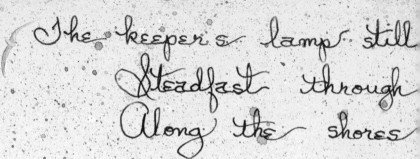

The keeper's lamp still
Steadfast through
Along the shores

O may the Holy Spirit
enable us to keep the
beacon-fire blazing, to
warn you of the rocks,
shoals, and quicksands,
which surround you,
and may He ever guide
you to Jesus.

Charles Spurgeon

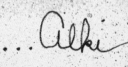
...Alki

...hines by day
the night
of Seattle ...

Give light,

and the darkness

will disappear of itself.

Erasmus

D. Morgan® © 2000

Point Light...

*Let your light shine before
men, that they may see your
good deeds and praise your
Father in heaven.*

The Book of Matthew

Through the storm . . .

D. Morgan © 1987

We must build our faith not on fading lights

but on the Light that never fails.

Oswald Chambers

..... You do not walk alone.

The Diamond by the Sea

Like a ruby in an antique brooch with sentiment untold,
The gem in the tower glistens with beauty to behold!
Its glow reflects where sea meets sand in sapphire rivulets
That trickle down with the ebbing tide to the ocean's treasure chest.

The jewel on the horizon worn with dignity and grace
Has romance and security wrapped up in its embrace.
Beneath the sky of topaz shining brilliantly
The lighthouse is the brightest gem—The Diamond by the Sea.

Author Unknown

From far away, a friendly light.

D. Morgan ©1994

Lord, help us be
a shining light
So others then may see
Your mercy and
Your love displayed
In what we strive to be.

David Sper

I have been here before
But when or how I cannot tell;
I know the grass beyond the door
The sweet keen smell
The sighing sound,
The lights around the shore.

Dante Gabriel Rossetti

His orchestration of the sea.

D. Morgan © 1998

a mesmerizing symphony.

The red light flamed on the white sails of a vessel gliding down the channel...Beyond her it smote upon and incarnadined the shining, white grassless faces of the sand dunes. To the right, it fell on the old house among the willows up the brook, and gave it for a fleeting space casements more splendid than those of an old cathedral.

L. M. Montgomery
Anne's House of Dreams

Lighthouses are unique expressions of human creativity. Physically, they represent triumphant solutions to complex engineering problems. Emotionally, they exemplify drama, rescue, poetry, romance, grandeur, nostalgia, and artistry.

Charles Wysocki

Guiding friendly strangers,
The Keeper
Of The Lighthouse

Is surely...

Thus does the lighthouse show
many things they otherwise
would not see, while it points
out the rocks on which the vessel
would suffer shipwreck.

Pope Pius X

D. Morgan ©1990

...*Friends with God.*

There is only one light
that never goes out.
It comes from God.
His light is the true light.

Stormie Omartian